'Permanent, Faithful, Stable'

'Permanent, Faithful, Stable'

Christian Same-Sex Marriage

Jeffrey John

DARTON·LONGMAN+TODD

First published in 1993 by
Darton, Longman and Todd Ltd
1 Spencer Court
140 – 142 Wandsworth High Street
London SW18 4JJ

New edition published in 2000

This edition published in 2012

ISBN: 978-0-232-52957-9

A catalogue record for this book is available
from the British Library.

Phototypeset by Kerrypress Ltd, Luton, Bedfordshire
Printed and bound by Bell & Bain, Glasgow

CONTENTS

FOREWORD

I was fortunate as a young priest to be encouraged by several clergy who taught me two things: that Anglican thinking about God has pastoral roots and that if this thinking ever challenges the past then it should be understood as a theological hoeing, a turning over of the soil of the tradition from which new things come to the top, and not as an arrogant discarding.

These clergy, in their various ways all theologians of experience, were loyal Christians whose pastoral work, as well as in some cases a costly self-scrutiny, had taught them important things they felt the institution of the Church found difficult to hear or even acknowledge — and yet must do, if it were to fulfil its vocation. Michael Mayne's engagement with HIV/AIDS patients at a time of widespread paranoid and judgmental commentary is a good example. Michael Mayne, John V. Taylor, Alan Ecclestone, Harry Williams, Bill Vanstone and Eric James were all amongst these priests who were so encouraging to me and, sadly, they have now all died. It is hard not to believe that something vital about the Anglican contribution to the Christian church has died with them.

I see this book by Jeffrey John very much as a similarly serious, Anglican and theological engagement with a simple fact that any pastor is only too aware of — that some people in every generation discover that they are

PREFACE

When I wrote the first version of this book, my aim was to show that there is only one possible theological and ethical framework for a same-sex partnership: that of permanent, faithful, stable monogamy. I also argued that this kind of relationship is what the great majority of gay people, like the great majority of heterosexual people, actually want and hope for. Most human beings, heterosexual or homosexual, know instinctively that a framework of secure, lasting, covenanted commitment maximises our chance of happiness and fulfilment. Almost all of us hope for someone who will be there for us, and who will stay with us 'till death us do part'. From a specifically Christian point of view, this model of human loving is best not only for practical reasons, but because a covenant of this kind between two people, whether of the same or different sexes, is in the image of God's own covenanted, constant love for us. It is sacramental because it helps make God's own kind of love visible in the world.

In 2005 this model of permanent, faithful, same-sex monogamy was officially endorsed and established in a scarcely hoped-for way by the introduction of civil partnerships. Since then same-sex couples in Britain have been able to contract a civil covenant which to all intents and purposes gives them the same legal protection and framework for life in society as heterosexual marriage. It is an act of legislation which has been almost universally acknowledged as a great good, a real advance for social stability and human happiness. Far more people entered civil partnerships than the government had forecast, and in the first years especially, a high proportion of them were older couples who had been together in secrecy or semi-secrecy for decades – some from before the time homosexual acts were decriminalised in 1967. The sense of release and liberation, of joy in a new-found sense of dignity and affirmation, was extraordinary. For gay Christians it was a cause of profound thanksgiving to God.

The official Church – and here my concern is mainly with the Church of England – is one of the few public domains where this development has been only grudgingly accepted and in some quarters vehemently opposed. In recent years, while society has moved towards acceptance, the Church has arguably moved in the opposite direction. In 1998, the Lambeth Conference declared homosexual practice to be 'incompatible with Scripture' in an atmosphere of perfervid homophobia which Bishop Richard Holloway compared to that of a Nuremberg Rally. When Archbishop George Carey was succeeded by Rowan Williams in 2002, most expected a change of approach, not least since Dr Williams himself had endorsed precisely the ethical framework for gay relationships described in this book, and had personally campaigned against the culture of lying about homosexuality that obtains in the Church. As Archbishop of Wales he had actually recommended this book in a letter to a friend as representing his own settled view on the matter. He wrote,

> By the end of the 80s I had definitely come to the conclusion that Scripture was not dealing with the predicament of persons whom we should recognise as homosexual by nature. I concluded that an active sexual relationship between two people of the same sex might therefore reflect the love of God in a way comparable to marriage, if and only if it had about it the same character of absolute covenanted faithfulness.

Tragically he changed his public position as soon as he reached the throne of St Augustine. Since then the Church's line on homosexuality has continued to harden. The Church of England has refused to countenance any form of official liturgical recognition for civil partnerships; has sought special exemptions from human rights and equalities legislation in order to continue discriminating against openly gay clergy or gay employees; has repeatedly restated its condemnation of all sexual relations outside heterosexual marriage; and has formally debarred even celibate gay clergy from becoming bishops. Most recently the bishops of the Church of England have set themselves hard against government proposals to extend civil marriage to include same-sex couples.

The chief motive for this regression is not any principled or consistent conviction about the wrongfulness of gay relationships. On the contrary, in private discussion and pastoral practice the majority of bishops, including both the present and the last Archbishop of Canterbury, have been personally supportive of gay relationships, and eager to say so. Their opposition to equal treatment is a public and political stance which is intended to maintain ecclesiastical unity, particularly within the Anglican Communion. About half the world's Anglicans are African, and the majority of them are in violently homophobic countries whose churches back harsh punishments against homosexuals, right up to the death penalty. These are the Anglican provinces which the current policy is seeking to appease and keep on board, while the American and Canadian Anglican churches which now openly bless gay unions and consecrate gay bishops are condemned for daring to treat gay people equally. This policy may be institutionally expedient, but it is morally contemptible. Worst of all, by appeasing their persecutors it betrays the truly heroic gay Christians of Africa who stand up for justice and truth at risk of their lives.

For the mission of the Church of England the present policy is a disaster. The Conservative Party realised ten years ago that the equal treatment of gay people had become a litmus test of basic human decency, and changed its view; but it is a test that the Church still spectacularly fails. While the Church readily blesses the second and even third marriages of couples who scarcely ever darken its doors, it refuses its blessing to hundreds of its own faithful, clergy and laypeople, who wish to bring their love and commitment before God. Fearful of the very large number of gay clergy and bishops in its own ranks, the Church's employment and disciplinary practices regularly punish the truthful and reward the deceitful. Not only gay people are repelled by all this: many more people of straightforward goodwill who instinctively expect the Church to uphold justice and truth, are scandalised when it so obviously does not. If in recent years secularism has gained ground in Britain, with the demand that the Church must be disestablished and surrender its voice in national life, it is the 'gay issue' more than any other that has brought it about.

The divergence between Church and popular opinion is likely to widen further still in the near future. In the civic sphere there is still one major step to be taken towards full equality and acceptance. The Prime Minister has promised that by 2015 legal marriage will become available to same-sex couples in Britain, as it already is in a dozen other countries of Europe and America. Ideologically (and, so this book argues, theologically) there is practically no difference between civil partnership and marriage, since both rest on a similar covenant promise of permanent and exclusive commitment between two people. Popular instinct agrees: civil partnership is already widely referred to as marriage, and the partnership ceremony as a 'wedding'. Many feel however that the official distinction of terms signifies and helps perpetuate a distinction in status: if marriage is the gold standard, civil partnership, though analogous to marriage, will always be seen as something less.

I agree, which is why I have changed the title of this book to 'Permanent, Faithful, Stable': Christian Same-Sex Marriage. When I first wrote it, I took the view that it was a matter of indifference whether the term 'marriage' was used for a monogamous Christian same-sex partnership or not: all that mattered was that the relationship was accorded the same ethical and sacramental status as Christian marriage. Theoretically that may still be true; but it is already obvious from the Church's very hostile reaction to the prospect of gay marriage that equivalent status will never become a reality until the term marriage is legally applied. Gay monogamy needs to be called marriage officially, as it already is instinctively and unofficially by many people, not simply because it must be seen to be equal, but because it must be seen to be equally holy, equally a gift and vocation of God to those who are called to it.

Here is a prediction. When civil gay marriage becomes possible the Church will initially continue to refuse to accept it, but will call for the continued availability of civil partnerships, so that it can offer gay people a second-best while reserving the term marriage for heterosexuals. In statements opposing gay marriage the Church's official spokesmen have already begun to praise the benefits of civil partnership, having conveniently forgotten that the civil partnership legislation only passed despite opposition from most bishops in the House of Lords. Civil partners will no doubt soon be offered a service of 'dedication' of the same sort that divorced heterosexuals used to be offered when a full Church marriage was denied to them. Already the demand for such a liturgy is growing among clergy, who are embarrassed by having to withhold the Church's official support from so many of their own flock who are in civil partnerships.

It will take much longer for the Church to come round to solemnizing same-sex marriage. But it will. The question is only how long it will take, and how much more damage we shall have to suffer on the way. The sadness is that the Church will, yet again, only get there reluctantly, following the State, and will finally realize much too late that the impulse which brought this about was truly God's impulse, even though it had to begin outside the Church. As with the equality of women, as with the emancipation of slaves, the thing which at first was supposed to be incompatible with Scripture and tradition will finally be seen to be demanded by the heart of the Christian Gospel itself. That is how it so often has been; but how bizarre that so few see it in advance. As Jim Cotter wrote twenty years ago:

> There are four stages in the Church's response to any challenge to its tradition. First, it pretends the challenge isn't there, Secondly it opposes it vehemently. Thirdly, it starts to admit extenuations and exceptions. Finally it says, 'That's what we really thought all along'.

What follows is the text of 'Permanent, Faithful, Stable' as printed in 2003, with only the most obvious anachronisms amended. The fact that there are so few of these shows, sadly, how little we have progressed in the Church – though not in civil society, thank God – in that time.

Jeffrey John
St Albans 2012

INTRODUCTION

This book has a straightforward aim. It argues that homosexual relationships should be accepted and blessed by
the Church, provided that the quality and commitment
of the relationship are the same as those expected of a
Christian marriage. It argues that the theological, ethical
and sacramental status of such a partnership between
two men or two women is comparable to that of a
marriage, whether or not the word marriage is used to
describe it. It also argues that the self-discipline and
self-sacrifice which are required to make Christian marriage a way of holiness are equally required of a homosexual partnership which deserves the name Christian.

The title of this book *'Permanent, Faithful, Stable'* is
taken from the description of such a relationship in the
Gloucester Report of 1979. This was the first Church of
England report – though it was never officially ratified –
to urge recognition of gay relationships by the Church.
The phrase has become something of a cliché but it says
what needs to be said about the kind of relationship I
want to defend.

The view which is put forward in this book tends to
draw fire from both sides of the argument.

On the one hand, many Christians, perhaps still the
majority, hold on the grounds of Scripture and tradition
that no kind of homosexual practice is compatible with

Christian discipleship. This is the official view of the Roman Catholic Church, the Orthodox Church and most of the Protestant Churches (though it is important to distinguish the official view from the private view of the leadership of these Churches, especially in the West). The Lambeth Conference of the Bishops of the Anglican Communion in 1998 also confirmed that traditionally negative stance and declared that all homosexual practice is 'incompatible with Scripture'. The Lambeth Conference of 2008, in an atmosphere of bitter division over the issue, did not alter that stance. Lambeth Conference resolutions, however, are not binding on member churches. The official position of the Church of England is expressed in the Statement *Issues in Human Sexuality*, published by the English bishops in 1991 and belatedly endorsed by General Synod in 1997. The Statement is a more nuanced document, which at certain points hovers on the edge of acceptance, urging congregations to accept and support Christians who conscientiously believe themselves to be called to live in faithful partnership. However, the overall tone remains hesitant and grudging, insisting that a gay relationship 'falls short' of the ideal of Christian marriage; and for this reason the Statement forbids such a relationship to clergy, because of their 'exemplary' role. Since *Issues in Human Sexuality* remains the most authoritative pronouncement to date in the Church of England on the subject of homosexuality, it will be referred to fairly frequently in what follows.

On the other hand, the view put forward in this book has been opposed by some gay people, including some of the most active and vocal, who think that for

homosexuals to adopt a monogamous model of relationship (sometimes dismissed as 'coupledom') is an inappropriate aping of heterosexual marriage. In more recent
years, partly because of the threat of AIDS, the idea and
practice of exclusive partnership and sexual fidelity have
gained more currency in gay circles. Long-term same-
sex partnerships are much more visible in the media, and
an increasing number of countries are according them
civil and legal recognition – by 2012 a dozen countries in
the world had legalised same-sex marriage. Andrew Sullivan, one of the most intellectually substantial of contemporary gay writers, argued powerfully in the nineties
for gay – and straight – monogamy on psychological,
social and political grounds, but his views were strongly
contested in gay circles. In the past even gay Christian
organizations were unwilling to formulate a monogamous ethic. This reluctance was certainly due in part to
the negative image of marriage for some gay people,
perhaps especially among lesbians, for whom the concept of monogamy often seems to carry an inseparable
connotation of male dominance. Perhaps another reason
is an instinctive fear of seeming to apply 'rules' when the
Church's and society's rules have for so long been unjust
and repressive.

So I have to argue on two fronts.

First, I want to help convince the mainstream Church
that a faithful homosexual relationship is not 'incompatible with Scripture' – certainly no more so than the
remarriage of the divorced, or the leadership of women,
which are far more 'incompatible' with the Bible's plain-
est meaning. I want to make it clear that accepting such a

relationship does not mean jettisoning the traditional biblical theology of sex and marriage, but rather extending it to include gay people – just as the sacrament of holy order has been extended in the Church of England to include women without at all changing our underlying theology of ministry. What makes a marriage sacramental is its nature as a faithful covenant, which expresses God's likeness in us and reflects the love between Christ and his Church. I want to persuade all Christians that a same-sex partnership based on the same commitment is no less sacramental a way of holiness and no less worthy of the Church's blessing.

At the same time I want to persuade gay people that contrary to traditional assumptions, the Gospel has something positive to say about gay relationships and those who live in them belong in the Church as much as anyone else. I want to point out that the sacramental theology which underlies the Church's teaching about sex and marriage applies to all human beings made in God's image, not only to heterosexuals. This theology says that human sexuality is not exclusively or necessarily intended for procreation; it is also intended to express a covenant commitment between two people which is holy because it reflects God's covenanted love for us, and gives us a framework for learning to love in his image. It means that for two people, whether of the same or different sexes, to live in such a faithful covenant with each other is a way to great freedom and growth, not a death-dealing rule. I want to hold out the hope, inspiration and moral challenge that such an understanding implies. I also want to strengthen Christian gay couples who already understand this, and know that their relationship is God's gift and vocation for them, but have to struggle to stay in a Church which repeatedly insults and rejects them.

I would not dare to write about Christian same-sex monogamy if I did not know it works. What I am writing derives as much from personal and pastoral experience as from theological reflection. Knowledge of many gay relationships based on this kind of Christian model has proved to me that it is not naïve or impracticable. Observation of what happens without such a model has convinced me that it is indispensable. Of course there is no such thing as the perfect Christian gay relationship, any more than one can point to the perfect heterosexual Christian marriage. One of the wiser things Archbishop Runcie said in the infamous General Synod debate of 1987 was that 'in this earthly tabernacle of Christ's kingdom there are many mansions, and all of them are made of glass'. The truth is that in matters of sex and human relationship, heterosexual or homosexual, all of us 'fall short of the ideal'.

But that does not mean we should abandon the ideal, or pretend that it does not exist, or worse still, deny it to others. For most of my ministry I have worked with young adults in secular and theological colleges and with young clergy. Many of them have been lesbian or gay, and many of them desperately struggling to reconcile their sexuality with membership of a hostile or uncomprehending Church. Almost all of them rejected promiscuity, and feared the futile prospect of a series of abortive relationships leading to a lonely old age. What they wanted was, precisely, the ideal: the hope, like their heterosexual friends, of finding someone to love and be wholly given to, someone to grow together with, some-one who would still be there at the end of the day and at the end of their life. That is not a heterosexual hope or a homosexual hope; it is a fundamental human hope. To deny and subvert that hope is simply inhumane, and utterly un-Christian. I am writing this because I believe we have an absolute duty in the Church to offer homo-sexual couples not only practical support, but the same theological understanding of their relationship that we offer to heterosexual couples, to help them fulfil the same hope, the same ideal – of permanent, faithful, stable love.

1

IS IT SCRIPTURAL?

'Incompatible with Scripture'? Use and Abuse of the Bible

I have a vivid memory of spending an unhappy afternoon over a Bible many years ago, trying to talk Simon out of attempting suicide again. Simon was a gay Evangelical student in a college where I was Chaplain, totally convinced on the basis of Romans 1 that if he ever succumbed to his feelings he would be damned. He had consulted the vicar of his own church, who had promptly prayed for 'healing' and simultaneously ordered him to give up helping in the Sunday School, 'to protect the little boys'. Not surprisingly, Simon had come back to college and swallowed half a bottle of pills. It was particularly tragic for him, and still is for many gay Evangelicals, that so many would-be 'Bible Christians' seem to have made a hard line on this issue practically a test of faith. Fortunately, some Evangelicals are now protesting against this line, but a great deal of damage is still being done.

It is important to see how damaging it is to use the Bible to condemn homosexuals in this way. It is equally important to see how arbitrary and selective it is, and how false is the claim to genuine biblical authority. In a notorious pronouncement the Lambeth Conference of 1998 embraced exactly this kind of selective fundamentalism by declaring that all homosexual acts are 'incompatible with Scripture'. What can this phrase mean? As we shall see, Scripture's teaching on homosexuality is sparse and ambiguous and it is highly questionable to what extent we can derive from it any application to the ethical issue of gay relationships as it faces us today. Yet this consideration did not prevent the bishops from issuing their blanket condemnation.

Contrast another ethical issue: that of divorce and remarriage. In four Gospel passages we are told that Jesus himself forbade the remarriage of the divorced as being equivalent to adultery. There is no doubt about the meaning of the words used, nor is there any indication that Jesus intended this teaching to be temporary or 'contextually interpreted'. On the contrary, it is a teaching he explicitly derives from God's plan in creation, and it is unambiguously expressed. Nothing of remotely equivalent weight and authority is stated in Scripture against homosexuality. How is it, then, that the Lambeth bishops can deny legitimacy, let alone blessing, to a faithful same-sex relationship on supposedly 'scriptural' grounds, yet, in the case of the great majority, are willing to bless remarried couples, and in some cases are divorced and remarried themselves? On what possible hermeneutical principle is 'incompatibility' discovered in the one case, yet not in the other? Let me emphasize that I do not use this example of remarriage in order to defend a literalist view on either issue. I use it because it demonstrates clearly that the bishops' declaration was based on prejudice, not on any consistent approach to biblical authority.

Similarly, why are so many Christians eager to take at face value what Paul says about homosexuals, but not what he says about women? Paul seems in three places (two only in passing) to condemn homosexual practice as sin. He has a great deal more to say about women. Consider his plain command that women must wear a head covering in church as a sign of their subordination; that women must be silent in the churches 'for they are not permitted to speak but must be silent as even the Law says'; that no woman may teach or hold authority over men, 'for Adam was formed first, then Eve; and Adam was not deceived, but the woman was deceived and became a transgressor. Yet woman will be saved through childbearing ...'. In the social circumstances of today these passages, which are so plainly degrading to women are highly embarrassing to 'Bible-based' churches. Paul himself lays far more stress on them than on his references to homosexuals. Yet in practice few even of the most so-called biblical churches now feel able to enforce the veiling of women or keep them silent.

If challenged on this, biblical conservatives employ exactly the sort of arguments which on other matters, not least homosexuality, they condemn as 'getting round the plain meaning of Scripture' or 'capitulating to the spirit of the age'. In the case of Paul's teaching about women they have to admit, when forced to the point, to making a distinction between temporary, 'culturally conditioned' teaching in certain passages, and wide biblical principles of justice and love with which those texts are now felt to conflict. Or else they will argue that Paul's teaching on women was conditioned by special circumstances in the churches he was writing to (though in fact more than once Paul says his teaching about women is binding on all the churches). The point to press home is that on such an issue even hard-line fundamentalists have been forced by outside moral pressure to recognize that certain biblical teachings must sometimes be weighed against other biblical principles and changed social conditions, and must sometimes be set aside. The sad truth is, the reason this has happened in the case of women and not in the case of homosexuals is that whereas prejudice against women is now much less tolerated in society at large, prejudice against homosexuals is still very much in force.

Sodom

Because so many Christians, even from Catholic and liberal traditions, still approach Scripture with essentially fundamentalist instincts, it is important to keep emphasizing that one cannot derive ethical instruction from the Bible texts without regard to their social and historical context and without weighing them against the thrust of Scripture as a whole. For example, even now one often hears the Sodom story (Genesis 19) brought into the Christian arguments about homosexual practice. Yet, as has been shown many times, the story has no relevance whatsoever to the ethical issues surrounding homosexual relationships, and never did.

In the original story the 'sin of Sodom' for which God had already decided to destroy the city before the events at Lot's house is unspecified. The sin committed by all the men of Sodom at Lot's house was one of gang rape by a majority of (presumably) heterosexual men. The homosexual element in the act held no particular interest for the author (the violation of hospitality would have been counted a far worse category of crime). Indeed, for centuries afterwards the 'sin of Sodom' was perceived not as homosexuality but as the contravention of the rules of hospitality, as it was clearly understood by Jesus himself in Matthew 10:14–15.

The identification of the sin of Sodom with homosexuality was first made by Jewish commentators in the period between the Testaments, who had a special interest in condemning homosexuality as a typically Gentile vice. It was they who bequeathed to subsequent generations the quite false notion that God destroyed Sodom because of homosexuality, together with the offensive vocabulary of 'sodomy', 'sodomite', etc. One should also point out that it would be very strange for us to derive ethical guidance and moral insights from such a primitive story, a story in which it is assumed to be perfectly right for Lot to offer his two daughters to be raped by the crowd as substitutes for his male guests (Genesis 19:8). In such texts as this the situation is far too remote from our own in human terms for any ethical transfer to be made.

Leviticus

Something similar must be said about the prohibition of male homosexual behaviour in the Holiness Code of Leviticus, where it is punishable by death (18:22, 20:13).

This is the earliest prohibition in Scripture, probably dating from the exile in Babylon, and it seems to have been conditioned by two main factors. First was the author's special concern to encourage childbirth in the situation of the exile and the forthcoming resettlement of Israel. (Probably the same author, known as the Priestly Writer, wrote the creation story in Genesis 1 with its command to 'go forth and multiply'.) Second was the need to counter syncretism by distinguishing sharply the ways of the Jews from those of the Gentiles. Babylonian society was apparently particularly tolerant of homosexual practice, and its worship may have involved homosexual activity. So by the ban on homosexuality the religious leaders of Israel sought to separate Jews from their Gentile captors – perhaps in more ways than one. It seems to have been this author who first labelled homosexuality as a particularly Gentile sin, and the abhorrence of it as a marker of Jewishness. Thereafter it becomes standard in Jewish literature to present homosexuality as characteristic of Israel's Gentile oppressors, and 'unknown in Israel'.

The Holiness Code is all about what sets Israel apart as holy to the Lord, but it is highly selective to single out homosexuality from the whole list of different activities which it condemns as 'abominations' – a list which includes, for example, the trimming of one's beard, the consumption of shellfish and the weaving of two different kinds of yarn into the same garment. Ethical derivation here can only be very highly selective. Of themselves the Levitical rules are in practice never regarded as having moral force for Christians, and Christians are not accustomed to look to them for guidance – except when seeking a text with which to beat homosexuals.

Jesus

It is often said, and it is true, that the Gospels never mention homosexuality. Jesus is not reported as ever having spoken about it. However there is one miracle story which may well have bearing on the subject – the healing of the centurion's servant, reported in Matthew 8:5–13 and Luke 7:1–10. It has long been recognised that the healing miracles of Jesus have a theological meaning far beyond being a simple demonstration of Jesus' divinity and power to heal. In particular, in a society where whole classes of people with various medical or social disabilities could be counted as 'non-kosher', 'unclean', and excluded from normal social and religious life under the laws of purity, the Gospels seem to show Jesus deliberately healing at least one in all the main categories of the excluded – lepers, cripples, menstruating women, others who were handicapped in various ways, Samaritans, Gentiles, tax collectors, prostitutes, the demon-possessed, the dead ... All of these were considered to be unclean and therefore unacceptable or defective in God's sight, and they were literally untouchable, since the impurity was regarded as being physically communicable to others. The theological point of the healing miracles is therefore to show Jesus not only healing the sick but including in his kingdom all these categories of people who under the law were supposed to be excluded, and who according to

Leviticus were even considered hateful to God. Jesus comes to declare that all these poor and marginalised, these despised and rejected, so far from being hateful to God, are in fact especially loved by him. Contrary to all the suppositions of the religious, they are the ones to whom the Kingdom especially belongs. The healing miracles demonstrate that 'inclusiveness', so far from being a trendy invention of modern liberalism, is at the very heart of Jesus' ministry and is demanded by the Gospel itself.

Both the centurion and his servant would certainly count as unclean and despised. Not only were they Gentiles, they were members of a hated foreign army that held the Jews in subjection. No pious Jew could have entered their house without making himself unclean too. The centurion acknowledges the fact with great humility: 'Lord I am not worthy that you should come under my roof'. However Gerd Theissen and other scholars have pointed out that there is a further aspect to their uncleanness and unacceptability. Any Jew encountering them, or reading the Gospel story about them, would almost certainly have assumed they were gay lovers. Homosexuality was portrayed by Jews of the time as an exclusively Gentile interest, and the charge of homosexual practice, especially directed against the occupying forces, was part of conventional and frequent Jewish polemic against the Romans. There is also plenty of evidence about Roman military life to show that the charge was often true. Domestic servants or orderlies were often chosen by officers on this basis, and some relationships were famously durable (the emperor

Hadrian and Antinous being perhaps the best-known couple). The centurion's deep concern, and especially the statement in Luke's version that the servant was 'very dear' to him, would have strengthened suspicion.

As Theissen pointed out, the possibility that the relationship was homosexual would not have escaped Jesus, Matthew or Luke. In view of Jesus' revolutionary inclusion of so many other categories of people who were declared to be 'unclean' or 'abominable' under the Levitical rules, it is a real question whether we are intended to see Jesus deliberately including a gay couple here as yet another category of the despised and rejected. Certainly there is no sign in the Gospel of anything but approval on Jesus' part for the centurion and his humble faith, nor is there any hint of 'Go and sin no more' after his servant is restored to him.

Paul

The only other relevant texts in Scripture are all in letters written by Paul or attributed to him. In 1 Corinthians 6:9 and 1 Timothy 1:10 homosexuality is mentioned in passing within conventional sin-lists, probably taken over from Hellenistic Jewish sources. (Both Hellenistic and Palestinian Judaism perpetuated the Levitical attitude to homosexuality as a Gentile vice, associated with the worship of pagan gods, and made extensive use of it as a piece of religious and political propaganda.) There is some reason to think that the words which we translate as 'homosexual' in these verses imply male prostitution, but this cannot be pressed. What is far more important is to remember that in the society in which Paul lived prostitution and pederasty (in the sense of the Greek practice of a temporary pupil-tutor relationship between a teenager and an older man) were the standard forms of homosexual practice, and these are the forms which were likely to be uppermost in Paul's mind when he refers to homosexuals. One cannot fairly make an ethical transfer from the assumptions behind these verses to the kind of equal, adult relationship which I am trying to defend in this book. Although he could have been theoretically aware of it, there is every reason to suppose that the practical possibility of such a relationship never entered Paul's thinking.

The most significant biblical text mentioning homosexuality is the one which drove Simon to despair: Romans 1:18ff. This needs more attention because it is by far the most important text to be considered, and the only place where we have anything like a theological argument against homosexual practice. However, the subject of homosexuality is not Paul's real interest here. The epistle is addressed to a church composed of both Jewish and Gentile converts. From Romans 1:18 to the end of the chapter Paul is engaged in an attack on Gentile idolatry. He argues that all people could have deduced knowledge of God from observing his creation, but they chose to reject that knowledge and turned to idol worship (v.23). Because of this perverse rejection of him, therefore God abandoned them to their lusts and impurity (v.24), to dishonourable passions exemplified in the exchange of heterosexual intercourse for homosexual (v.25), and to a base mind and improper conduct, exemplified in a long list of sins deserving death which closes the chapter (vv. 28–32). This completes the attack on the Gentiles. The tables are then turned at the start of chapter 2, where Paul rounds on the Jews in his audience (who may well have been applauding smugly up to this point) to condemn them equally for the same sins, although they had even less excuse, having the Law. The rhetorical pattern is carefully constructed, and reaches its climax in chapter 3 with the fundamental proclamation that Paul wants to impress on Gentiles and Jews alike: that all have sinned, none is righteous, but all can be justified through the atoning sacrifice of Jesus Christ.

The rhetorical force of the exercise lies in Paul's quoting back at the Jews their own conventional propaganda against the Gentiles. As we have noted, both Palestinian and Hellenistic Judaism portrayed homosexuality as an exclusively Gentile vice. In Hellenistic Judaism especially, the homosexuality to which the Gentiles are supposed to incline is conventionally related to their idolatry, the moral 'exchange' of one sex for another being seen as the direct result of the religious 'exchange' of the true God for an idol. Paul repeats this standard argument; in fact several verses in the Book of Wisdom chapters 13 and 14 are sufficiently close to make borrowing a real possibility, and there are also parallels in Philo, Josephus and the Testament of the Twelve Patriarchs.

Of course the fact that Paul borrowed a piece of conventional anti-Gentile polemic need not undermine the authority of what he says, but there is another important point to be made about the presuppositions of his argument. When Paul argues that homosexuality is 'against nature' he does not only mean that it is against the order of nature itself, but also that it is against the person's *own* nature. Like all earlier and contemporary Jewish (though not all classical) writers on the subject, Paul does not recognize a separate category of homosexual people but only homosexual acts. He takes it for granted, like all the rest of biblical literature, that homosexual behaviour is a free, perverse choice on the part of 'naturally' heterosexual men and women. This assumption is perfectly clear in his statements that homosexuals 'gave up' or 'exchanged' heterosexual relations in verses 26 and 27. It is also essential to his portrayal of homosexuality as an instance and reflection of idolatry. He *must* believe that homosexuals wilfully choose their unnatural aberration in the same way that he *must* believe that idolaters wilfully suppress the truth about God that *must* be known to them from observing creation (1:18–19). Otherwise, as he says, God would not be just in his condemnation, and Paul could not say they are without excuse.

Yet we know now that this fundamental assumption on Paul's part is quite false. His belief that homosexual acts are committed by 'naturally' heterosexual people is untrue. There are quite clearly those whose exclusive or predominant inclination, whether for genetic reasons or for reasons of upbringing, is unarguably and unchangeably towards their own sex. And as Paul himself admits, if men and women had no choice in the matter, God would hardly be just in condemning them. We may well agree with him, and observe that this false assumption on his part wholly undermines any blanket condemnation of homosexual practice on the basis of Romans 1.

It is, then, these two considerations: (1) that the object of Paul's condemnation was the model of homosexual practice in Hellenistic society, namely prostitution or pederasty, and (2) that neither Paul nor his Jewish antecedents considered that case of a homosexually orientated person, that make it thoroughly unjust and inappropriate to wield these texts against the kind of relationship I am seeking to defend.

Creation and Natural Law

Some will still argue that even a relationship of this quality must be condemned on the ground of Paul's so-called natural law objection that it is against the God-given pattern of creation. In an article defending this position one writer sums up such an argument with the apocalyptic comment that 'to accept homosexual acts by inverts would be deny the doctrine of creation … the whole biblical teaching on creation, sex, marriage, forgiveness and redemption will be fundamentally altered' (G. Wenham).

So let us consider the biblical argument from creation. What, scripturally speaking, is the purpose of sex? What was God's will in creating male and female? One might have assumed childbirth, but, surprisingly perhaps, in Genesis itself the primary reason that God created a companion for Adam is not said to be procreation, but because 'God said, "It is not good for man to be alone" ' (2:18). Complementarity and companionship are at least as much a part of God's plan in creation as childbirth. Indeed it is remarkable that in the Genesis account childbirth emerges only as an afterthought, and in the rather negative context of God's punishment of Eve (3:16). It is highly significant that Jesus and Paul, while both referring to the creation story, never once mention procreation or physical sexual difference in their teaching about marriage. On the contrary, their stress is entirely on the quality of the relationship, and in particular that it should be a covenant of total sexual fidelity and indissoluble union. Furthermore, the insistence on fidelity is never explained, as we might expect, with reference to practical reasons of child-bearing or domestic stability, but always with reference to the personal and spiritual implications of sexual union.

For Paul, sexual union *always* has spiritual consequences, whether for good or ill. Promiscuous sexual activity involves desecration of the body, which is a temple of the Spirit and itself a member of the Body of Christ (1 Corinthians 6:15-20). But where sexual union expresses mutual love and commitment, that relationship becomes a *mysterion* (Ephesians 5:32), a holy mystery or sacrament which reflects the covenant union of the faithful love between Christ and the Church, and which itself becomes a channel of love and grace in the world. For each human being to make such a covenant is for him or her to realize an important part of what it means to be made in God's image. It means to further his primary and ultimate purpose in creation by reproducing the kind of creative (but not necessarily procreative) self-giving love that is basic to God's own nature. Accepting homosexual relationships does not mean jettisoning this fundamental biblical teaching about the sacramental character of human sexuality.

Those who continue to cling to a natural law argument against homosexuality on the basis of Romans 1 should also be reminded that Paul appeals more frequently and clearly to natural law and the creation story in order to justify his now abandoned teachings about the veiling and silencing of women. Paul said that women must be veiled because man was created first and it is primarily man who is the image of God (1 Corinthians 11:7–8). It is shameful for a man to wear long hair and a woman to wear short hair because 'nature itself teaches so' (1 Corinthians 11:14; a much clearer expression of 'natural law' than anything in Romans 1). No woman is permitted to teach or to hold authority over men and women are commanded to be silent 'because Adam was formed first, then Eve; and Adam was not deceived but the women was deceived and became a transgressor' (1 Timothy 2:12–14). These are theological arguments which appeal to God's plan in creation no less than Romans 1:18ff., and indeed Paul is much clearer about their authoritative status and the practical rules he intends to deduce from them, even to the point of saying the silencing of women is a command of the Lord, and if anyone disputes it he is to be rejected (1 Corinthians 14:33–8). It is obvious that Paul lays far more weight of doctrine and authority on this teaching about women than on his passing references to homosexuality. Yet the fact that today it is consistently ignored, even in the most traditional churches, is not felt to 'deny the doctrine of creation' or 'to alter fundamentally the whole biblical teaching on creation, sex, marriage, forgiveness and redemption'.

I remarked that the original biblical prohibition of homosexuality was probably written in the situation of the Babylonian exile, as a mark of Jewish separateness from the surrounding culture. Babylon remains a powerful symbol for modern secular society, and in one sense it might fairly be argued that the situation of Christians has *not* changed. As 'aliens and exiles' Christians still understand themselves to be called, no less than the Jews in Babylon, to a distinctive morality and distinctive holiness which will challenge the world in sexual matters as in all else (1 Peter 2:3). This is not to be denied. The point is that the most distinctive and constructive witness that homosexual Christians can offer, both to 'Babylon' in the shape of the secular gay scene and to the Church itself, is the witness of relationships marked by the same quality of holy and faithful love to which heterosexual Christians are called in marriage.

◼

2

IS IT MORAL?

More Natural Law

If the person in the street objects to homosexual practice, the chances are that the objection will be based first
of all on a common-sense form of the natural law argument similar to Paul's in Romans 1. Homosexuality does
not seem to fit the observed order of nature. There are,
after all, two sexes – to quote the well-worn *bon mot* of
Anita Bryant, God made Adam and Eve, not Adam and
Steve. There is also an argument from design. Our genital
equipment exists primarily for procreation, and in gay
sex procreation is not a possibility. More fundamentally,
two male or two female bodies simply do not fit together
in the same way as a male and a female. In particular
some objectors have a very strong instinctive reaction
against the 'unnaturalness' of anal sex – though of course
this is not the only, or even the predominant, form of
homosexual activity, and like all forms of homosexual
activity, it also occurs among heterosexuals.

Some statements of the natural law argument are
plainly wrong. One of the oldest is in Plato (though he
himself did not hold to it): that because homosexual
activity does not occur among animals, it ought not to be
done among humans either. Here the basic premise is
simply mistaken: homosexual activity is in fact common

to very many classes of animals, and in this sense is therefore perfectly 'natural'. But there is a more important consideration that tells against the natural law argument in general. The truth is that in other matters we do not regulate our behaviour or derive our moral precepts simply from observation of what nature does or does not do. Civilization itself depends on our disobeying many instincts and urges which might be termed 'natural'. We are constantly re-inventing, adapting, manipulating and often reversing the ways of the natural world in order to serve what seems to us a higher good, a better 'law'. At this level the natural law argument against homosexuality has as much force as the early objection to aviation on the grounds that 'if God had meant us to fly he'd have given us wings'.

More specifically, in managing nature we do not usually have qualms about adapting, altering or reversing natural bodily processes and functions in order to prolong or enhance life. Medicine and surgery are obvious examples. We intervene to maximize the capacities of our bodies and the health and wholeness of our lives. Even if one were to accept the demeaning view of homosexuality as a disorder or handicap, we do not condemn the 'handicapped' for adapting and using in the best and most creative way possible the gifts and capacities which they possess. One rather applauds and supports them. Those who claim to be repelled and disgusted by homosexual forms of intercourse might ask why they are not disgusted by a painter who expresses his creativity by painting with his feet, or by an author who types by blowing down a tube. They should also, of course, ask themselves whether they object to similar sexual acts between heterosexuals and if not, why not. I would reject the term 'handicap' for homosexuality, except in so far as gay people are handicapped by other people's prejudices; but I believe there is a true analogy between the homosexual's so-called 'unnatural' use of his or her physical equipment to make love and these examples of the 'unnatural' use of the body to make art.

It is worth noting here that the long and unresolved 'nature versus nurture' debate as to the cause of homosexuality, although it is constantly raised, has no proper bearing on the discussion of the morality of homosexual practice. Campaigners for the acceptance of gay relationship have tended to insist on a genetic origin, on the grounds that it would seem to confirm that homosexuality is a 'given' of creation, and therefore 'natural' and willed by God. Thinking along the same lines of a false natural law argument, opponents have tended to see it as a psychological disorder, due to parental or other 'mistakes', and therefore attributable to human failure and not to the will of God. However, even if the origin of homosexuality could be shown to be either genetic or psychological (and it is just as likely to be both), that still would not tell us whether the phenomenon of homosexuality is good or bad, willed by God or not. Genetic conditioning produces good things and bad things, things like the wonderful diversity of races and features and capacities, which we believe is part of God's will in creation, and things like congenital disease, which we believe is not. Equally our psychological conditioning can work for good or ill. What matters morally for all of us is not so much how we come to be what we are, but what we do with it.

The Purpose of Sex

Homosexual activity of course does not fit the natural pattern of procreation. But we are long past arguing – unless we are extremely conservative Roman Catholics – that sexual activity is only right and good when there is a possibility of childbirth. It is true that Anglican bishops condemned contraception on these grounds until 1930, but we can safely say that the position has now been abandoned. In any case, the idea that procreation was a necessary condition for moral sexual union was never logically or rigorously applied. Even the most conservative churches have generally accepted that sexual relations are permissible within marriages where one or both partners are infertile, or past the age of childbearing. This is clearly because within such a marriage sexual activity has always been perceived as good in itself, quite apart from any possibility of childbirth.

If we ask what are the legitimising purposes of sex in marriage, the Book of Common Prayer laid down three. First, it was for the procreation of children. Second, it was 'a remedy against sin, and to avoid fornication'. Third, it was 'for the mutual society help and comfort that the one ought to have of the other, both in prosperity and in adversity'. The marriage service in Common Worship, the Church of England's contemporary service book, puts the same thing rather more positively (and puts procreation last):

Marriage is a gift of God in creation through which husband and wife may know the grace of God. It is given that as man and woman grow together in love and trust, they shall be united with one another in heart, body and mind, as Christ is united with his bride, the Church. The gift of marriage brings husband and wife together in the delight and tenderness of sexual union and joyful commitment to the end of their lives. It is given as the foundation of family life in which children are [born and] nurtured, and in which each member of the family, in good times and in bad, may find strength, companionship and comfort.

With the exception of childbirth (which is in any case only conditionally included, as the square brackets show) all these purposes of marriage can be fulfilled in a permanent, faithful, stable gay relationship, and are being fulfilled in many. The case of an infertile heterosexual couple proves that the absence of the possibility of procreation cannot mean that the attempt to achieve all these other good purposes of God in creating sexual love thereby becomes immoral. The onus is therefore on those who reject homosexual relationships to show where the difference lies in moral status between an infertile marriage and a committed gay relationship. I do not believe that such a difference can in fact be shown.

Moral or Social Status?

At this point the person in the street may balk again. How can one claim that a gay or lesbian relationship is equivalent in status to a marriage? Professors of moral theology may balk too. In a letter I received from one of these, he declined to contribute to a projected book on the subject of homosexual monogamy. He explained that although he sympathized with the position I am putting forward here, he felt unable sincerely to defend equivalence between Christian marriage and a committed gay relationship, knowing that he would prefer his own children or grandchildren to be married than to take a same-sex partner.

Unfortunately the professor did not explain whether his preference was based on theology or instinct, but I strongly suspect the latter. In the first place, I have to be clear (and should have made it clear to the professor) that I am of course talking about an equivalence of Christian moral status or acceptability between marriage and gay partnership, not an equivalence of current social or personal desirability. If I had children, I expect I too would prefer them to marry, in the first place because I too would hope for grandchildren, and in the second place, because I would not wish on anyone who could avoid it the massive strain which is still imposed on gay relationships by others – and especially alas by other Christians. The inability to bear their own children (I mean the inability to bear children together, of course, in the case of lesbians) and the difficulty of adopting is a real cause of sadness for same-sex couples, as it is for heterosexual

couples who cannot have children. The continuing difficulty of sustaining a permanent, faithful, stable gay relationship in the present climate of Church and society is
not to be underestimated – though seeing this should
drive us to change, not accept the prejudices that make it
so. For these reasons I accept that at the practical level, a
gay relationship is disadvantaged as against a marriage.

But to be socially disadvantaged is not the same as to
be wrong or morally inferior. Even if a childbearing
marriage is seen as the 'best' in terms of its relative
chance of practical and personal fulfilment, that does not
make it the enemy of the good in the case of those for
whom the 'best' is not an option. On the contrary, as
even *Issues in Human Sexuality* recognizes, in such adverse
circumstances there are many homosexual couples

> who grow steadily in fidelity and in mutual car-
> ing, understanding and support, whose partner-
> ships are a blessing to the world around them, and
> who achieve great, even heroic sacrifice and devo-
> tion.

It is good to reach such an affirmation on the part of the
bishops, but it must be said that there is an odd disjunc-
tion between, on the one hand, this observation and the
positive tone of the first four chapters of *Issues,* and on the
other the conclusions drawn in the fifth chapter. It is
extraordinary that *Issues* in its first section appears to
accept the objections to the traditional arguments against
homosexual practice which I have outlined, yet at the end
simply restates the natural law argument in its crudest
form:

> Homophile orientation and its expression in
> sexual activity do not constitute a parallel and
> alternative form of human sexuality as complete
> within the created order as the heterosexual ...
> heterosexuality and homosexuality are not equally
> congruous with the observed order of creation ...

In the same section a homosexual relationship is also said
to be less 'valid' and 'not on a par with heterosexual
marriage as a reflection of God's purposes in creation'.

But if a homosexual relationship can be 'a blessing to
the world around', and 'a way of heroic self-sacrifice and
devotion', in what precise sense is it 'less valid' and
'unequal'? Apparently not in a moral sense, since the
bishops accept that a homosexual relationship can carry
these marks of holiness, and that it is the most constructive and positive thing that some individuals can do with
their own nature. They are also at pains to point out that
homosexuals are not to be devalued as people, and that to
categorize homosexuality as a sickness to be healed is
inappropriate, dangerous and degrading. So what kind of
inferiority is left? Once these possibilities are excluded,
the statement that homosexuality is not 'congruous with
the observed order of creation', seems to amount to no
more that the trivial observation that it is a minority
orientation and does not produce children. One might
point out that celibacy is equally a minority orientation
which does not produce children, and equally incongru-
ous with the observed order of nature, though for most
of its history the Church has tended to regard it as more
valid than, and indeed superior to, marriage.

It is hard to avoid the conclusion that the natural law objection has simply been re-imported at the end of *Issues*, just at the point where practical action has to be broached, in order to express what is really no more than my professor's undeniable and instinctive feeling that a homosexual relationship is less 'complete' (to use the bishops' word) because it cannot bear children, and less convenient because of social custom and other people's prejudice. If more than this is intended it needs clarifying, because I have not been able to find any other reason for the 'inequality' or 'lesser validity' in the document. Again I would focus on the question: does it imply any moral or religious or personal difference (i.e. any difference which is not the obvious physical one) between a committed gay relationship and an infertile marriage. If so, what is it?

Complementarity

One possible response might be to suggest that as well as having bodies which are designed to fit together in a particular way, the two sexes are also meant to fit together emotionally and mentally. So it is sometimes argued that homosexual relationships are wrong, and perhaps more likely to fail, because they lack the element of psychological complementarity which is supposedly an important feature of heterosexual relationships.

It seems to be scientifically provable that *in general* there are real differences between the psychologies of the two sexes. There is even some scientific evidence that these differences are traceable to different configurations in the male and female brain. The stereotypes are well known. Men are supposedly active, dominant, individualistic, aggressive and analytical, valuing theoretical thought and perception. Women are supposedly passive, social, bonding and nurturing, valuing instinctual thought and emotional perception ... and so on. There may be a certain practical value in perceiving these differences of collective generalizations, but we have rightly learned to be wary of them because we have seen that injustice and oppression invariably come in when these generalizations are imposed on individuals as normative rules. The feminist movement is a reaction against precisely this kind of oppression, and phenomena like the 'new man' concept or Robert Bly's 'men's movement' are equally a reaction against the imposition of 'macho' images and norms of behaviour on men. For this reason, in secular relationships, as in current pastoral theology, the emphasis has moved sharply from the distinction of gender norms to the equality of human persons, and so to an open and interchangeable complementarity of roles. Few Christians would now criticize a marriage in which, say, the wife was the principal earner and the husband stayed at home as nurturer. On the contrary, we might praise the couple's adaptability. Having reached this understanding, it would be highly unreasonable to continue to argue against a homosexual relationship on the grounds of a supposed incompatibility of stereotypes, when we no longer recognize those stereotypes as normative in marriage.

In fact, just as rigid stereotypes of masculinity and femininity are breaking down in marriage, it seems they are breaking down in homosexual partnerships too. Whereas in the past homosexuals typically adopted an active or passive role on the traditional model of marriage, Terry Sanderson, in a (mostly) admirable book called *Making Gay RelationshipsWork*, writes

> Research – and our own observations – have proved that 'butch-femme' scenario of gay relationships is rare these days, if not altogether extinct ... We are far more likely to base our relationships on the 'best friend' model, a far superior arrangement that produces an egalitarian framework within which to function. This has advantages over the traditional heterosexual model which frequently reduces the woman to the status of subordinate ... How many married women wish they could be best friends with their husband instead of being his drudge and servant?

An American psychological counsellor, T. Tessina, writing a similar book *Gay Relationships* for lesbians and gay men, also notes with approval that male-female role distinctions now tend to characterize only the relationships of more elderly lesbians. She advises – as any good marriage counsellor might – that even if a 'leader' role is more natural to one partner, and a more passive role to the other, the essential things is not to make the roles mutually exclusive or irreversible and never to take the other for granted.

It is obvious that any couple, homosexual or heterosexual, must find a way of living together which accords

with their own instincts and temperament (gender-
conditioned or otherwise) and which allows each of
them a fair share of freedom and responsibility. For any
couple this is a large part of learning to love and grow
together. In a fine and moving passage of *Issues* the bishops
say of marriage:

> A true marriage reflects Christ's own love for us
> all. He too gave himself to others 'for better or
> worse, till death'. In it we learn to break down
> our pride and self-concern, to be open to our
> partner as he or she really is, to treasure what is
> good, and forgive faults, to sacrifice ourselves for
> the sake of the other, to be loyal whatever the
> price ... A good marriage creates for each part-
> ner the same kind of environment which we
> recognize as promoting growth to maturity in the
> case of children: a combination of love and chal-
> lenge within an unbreakably reliable relationship.

Precisely the same is true of a gay relationship. In fact it is
striking to read how closely the bishops' portrait of a
good marriage resembles the secular recipe of Tessina
and Sanderson for successful gay and lesbian partnerships
– though they might all be very surprised to realize it.
The point is that personal 'sameness' and 'otherness' go
far beyond crude physiological or psychological distinctions. Ultimately all persons are uniquely made and
inescapably different; but marriage implies a common
will and common purpose in a shared life which tran-
scends and unites personal difference without obliterat-

ing it. It teaches us that we are not made for ourselves but for God and for one another, and helps us learn God's kind of love by practising the self-sacrifice to which the marriage covenant calls us. This is the mystery and joy of self-giving love, the ecstasy, *ek-stasis* – literally standing outside our self – by which we find our best and truest self by losing oneself in love for the other. In however faltering a way, it is what enables us to reflect the love between the Persons of God himself, and is a crucial aspect of our creation in God's image.

Friendship or Monogamy?

I have just quoted with approval the statement that in gay relationships the model of partnership is more often that of the best friend than that of marriage in the traditional heterosexual mould. But I believe it is a serious mistake, leading to serious moral consequences, to use the term 'friendship' as the primary term for a same-sex relationship. Of course it is true of both a heterosexual marriage and a committed gay partnership that the most successful relationship is likely to be one in which the couple are best friends as well as sexual partners. But in Christian doctrine a marriage, even considered apart from procreation, is far more than friendship, and the term friendship is wholly inadequate to cover what marriage and sexual commitment imply theologically. Friendship in any normal use of the term does not imply sexual activity, still less in any theological use, and it is an abuse to try to force it to do so. One may have many friends;

one may not, within any moral framework which remotely links with Christian teaching, have many sexual partners.

My rejection of the term 'friendship' as the appropriate term for any sexually-expressed partnership is opposed to the view of two of best-known Christian gay writers in Britain in recent years, Elizabeth Stuart and Michael Vasey. Vasey's book *Friends and Strangers* is a plea, written from the perspective of a gay Evangelical, for the inclusion of the gay Christian experience within the Church. His analysis of the biblical material relating to the issue is especially compelling and perceptive. Vasey does not attempt, however, to build a theological model for gay relationships or offer any moral framework for homosexual practice. Rather, by repeatedly asserting that 'there are no blueprints' for gay relationships and viewing them in contradistinction to heterosexual marriage, he effectively cuts gay people off from any positive theological self-understanding or moral guidance which the Christian tradition might offer. This leaves him apparently pleading for the Church to accept gay relationships on any terms whatever.

Elizabeth Stuart in her books *Daring to Speak Love's Name* and *Just Good Friends* sets out to develop a 'lesbian and gay theology of relationships' based entirely on the category of friendship. She insists most emphatically (and in this agrees with *Issues* and more recent pronouncements from the bishops) that lesbian and gay relationships are not marriage and that blessings of these relationships would not be weddings. Her rejection of the terms 'marriage' and 'monogamy' is based on the-view that these simply cannot be isolated from 'patriarchal' domination and abuse. On similar grounds she refuses any application of covenant theology to sexual relationships, regarding the prophets' description of the marriage between Yahweh and Israel, or the Pauline description of marriage as the 'mystery' of Christ and the Church, as being inextricably tied to assumptions of slavery and subjugation. In the later book she effectively rejects marriage itself as being inherently a tool of patriarchal control. Any attempt to gain acceptance of gay relationships on similar terms is therefore essentially misguided:

> What is the ultimate value of incorporation into an institution which even heterosexuals are asking serious questions about, an institution which was born, formed and structured for and by patriarchy? (*Just Good Friends* p 174)

Stuart admits that there may be some happy marriages, but only as it were by accident, when married people strive to 'subvert' the institution into something which it inherently is not.

Here is a gulf, probably unbridgeable, between Stuart's view and mine. Unlike Stuart, I do not despair of monogamy and continue to understand marriage as a gift of God and a sacrament of the Church. I do not accept that it is essentially and irredeemably patriarchal, even though it is undeniably bound up with patriarchy and male 'headship' in its origins and development. For all the criticism that can fairly be levelled at marriage as practised throughout history and in the present, inequality and injustice are not a necessary part of the institution, as many if not most contemporary marriages show. No one could deny the evils and injustices which marriage has meant for many, and especially for women. But *absus non tollit usum* – abuse does not argue for disuse; and *corruptio optimi pessima* – it is the corruption of the best which is the worst. A genuinely equal, happy and mutually affirming marriage is not such a rare phenomenon, and monogamy is still the framework within which the great majority of women and men choose to live their lives. Seen in this perspective, Stuart's attitude of total rejection, while it may be understandable from a particular lesbian and feminist standpoint, looks quite unreasonably negative and pessimistic.

This difference of view is a central issue for Christian sexual ethics today, far more crucial than the 'gay issue' alone. It is a fundamental question about human nature, about the way we are made and the way we can expect to find fulfilment. Is it true that the capacity to make a covenant of lifelong, committed, faithful love with one person is one of God's greatest gifts, a reflection in us of his own nature? Is it true that for most people it is the best framework for personal flourishing, the best in which *both* partners can grow to be *more* freely and fully themselves? Or is believing and attempting this no more than what Stuart calls 'the idolatry of the ideal', setting up a prison which in practice almost inevitably generates misery, guilt and abuse? Closely tied to this question is a second. How does the context of sexual activity relate to the wellbeing of the human person? Is it best if sexual intercourse happens only within and as an expression of, this kind of personal covenant? Or is sexual intercourse detachable from commitment, and the context in which it occurs a matter of moral and spiritual indifference?

In Stuart's view:

> There would seem to be nothing inherently wrong with friends who are not involved in relationships of radical vulnerability (i.e. of personal commitment) enjoying intimate physical relations, as long as these are negotiated honestly with all concerned. If we accept, as we surely must, that acts of physical intimacy have no inherent meaning, then the onus is on the friends to establish the boundaries of their relationship. (*Just Good Friends* p 224)

The most startling part of this statement is the throwaway line, 'If we accept, as we surely must, that acts of physical intimacy have no inherent meaning ...'. In Stuart's view, the meaning or meaninglessness of sexual activity entirely depends on context. She believes that, because 'there is no universal meaning to sex ... and genital contact is not "the ultimate" expression of closeness', then even anonymously promiscuous sex may be 'unproblematic'. The only moral criteria for sexual activity, even between total strangers, are consent, honesty and non-exploitation. I will say more about gay promiscuity in the next chapter. But it is worth observing here that for an author who accuses the church of dualism – that is, an unhealthy separation of body and soul – it is a remarkable assumption that what one does with one's body sexually can be regarded as detachable from and irrelevant to one's person.

Stuart claims to be offering an 'empirical theology', one based on her own knowledge of the secular gay subculture. But Christian theology is about more than describing 'what happens': it is an attempt to understand – and ultimately to redeem – 'what happens' in relation to profound truths about human nature revealed in Scripture and Christian tradition. The best Stuart can do in this respect is to try and find paradigms in Scripture and tradition for her model of sexually expressed friendship. Although she admits at one point that one cannot prove that any of these friendships involved sexual expression, she nevertheless repeatedly refers to David and Jonathan, Ruth and Naomi, Jesus and the beloved disciple, as if it *were* proved that they were sexually expressed. Similarly she calls on Aelred of Rievaulx in support, but Aelred, who was almost certainly homosexual himself, was perfectly clear that, though limited physical demonstrations of affection between particular monastic friends could be countenanced, sex could not – for the very practical reason that it would create division and destruction in the community. We know from Aelred's own writings that Stuart's notion of open sexual friendship was abhorrent to him, not simply because (as she believes) he had 'internalized the fears of his age', but more importantly because he knew from experience that *it does not work*: uncovenanted sex generates envy and instability, which in turn make community relationship impossible.

For similar reasons, although Stuart is right in accusing me of giving primacy to Scripture and tradition, I believe my own views are no less empirically and practically based than hers. Observation of 'what happens', both on the 'gay scene' and on the 'straight scene', leads me to believe very strongly that the Church's wisdom in advising men and women to confine sexual activity to permanent, faithful relationships, remains as wise as it ever was. On the firmly empirical basis of having picked up the pieces of too many damaged people, I am convinced that anonymous or 'recreational' sex is *never* 'unproblematic' or irrelevant to a person's emotional and spiritual health. On the contrary, quite apart from the guilt and fear which are usually involved, like other addictions it dulls the appetite for normal life, and creates a peculiar kind of introversion, a sense of inner exile which is ultimately destructive of real relationships. Paul's statement that sexual activity divorced from loving commitment 'tears away' part of the person, whether one wills it or not, is a matter of experience, not theological theory. The same holds true of sexually 'open' relationships. Honesty is a necessary, but hardly sufficient condition for a happy relationship, and in practice sexual envy and competition, fear of disease, fear of ageing, the cult of youth, the sense of being robbed of a partner's emotional and sexual energy, and above all the emotional insecurity of constantly wondering how much one is loved and for what and for how long – all contribute to instability and likely destruction.

Michael Vasey's insistence that there are 'no blueprints' for gay relationships, and Elizabeth Stuart's rejection of monogamy and endorsement of sexually open 'friendships', for all their Christian packaging, derive from an uncritical acceptance of the tenets of secular sexual liberationism. They give no clue as to what a distinctively Christian homosexual relationship might be. They offer no engagement with the deep mainstream of Christian teaching about the sacredness of sex or the importance of sexual discipline for personal integrity, and they leave gay people with no moral structure or guiding wisdom for building emotionally secure and sexually healthy lives. Their views, translated into behaviour, are physically as well as spiritual dangerous. It is worth pondering this judgement by Andrew Sullivan, whose own arguments for covenant monogamy are conditioned by his own close empirical knowledge of the American gay scene over the last ten years:

> The gay liberationists have plenty to answer for. For far too long they promoted the tragic lie that no avenue of sexuality was any better or nobler than any other; that all demands for responsibility or fidelity or commitment or even healthier psychological integration were mere covers for 'neoconservatism' or worse, 'self-hatred'; that even in the teeth of a viral catastrophe, saving lives was less important than saving a culture of 'promiscuity as a collective way of life', when, of course, it was little more than a collective way of death. They have demeaned gay men almost as surely as their unwitting allies, the fundamentalists. (*Love Undetectable*, p. 52)

3

IS IT ACHIEVABLE?

Promiscuity and Fidelity

Two courageous London priests pioneered blessing ceremonies for homosexual couples through the 1980s.
Though they are now joined by very many more, these
two have probably officiated at more such ceremonies –
together numbering some hundreds – than any other
clergy in the country. They testify that they have always
offered couples the choice of making temporary vows, or
vows, as in marriage, of permanent, lifelong faithfulness.
Both report that all but a tiny number have chosen to
make lifelong vows to one another. As far as these priests
can tell, the success rate of these couples in terms of
durability is high – certainly not lower than that of the
'normal' marriages which they also celebrated week by
week.

It is impossible now to repeat the old prejudice about
gay relationships that 'they can't last'. That lie was
silenced by the 18,000 gay couples who came forward in
the first year after the introduction of civil partnerships
in 2005, most of them having lived unofficially in committed monogamous relationships for many years. It is a
testimony to the reality and strength of the monogamous
instinct in all human beings that gay relationships could
succeed even despite the lack of any legal framework or

social support, despite the absence of the cohesive force of childrearing, and despite the constant undermining force of ecclesiastical and social hostility. When one remembers that even with all the support which church and society supply the success rate of heterosexual monogamy is unimpressive, the fact that so many gay relationships achieve permanence may seem little short of miraculous.

There is no reason to believe that homosexual men are naturally more inclined to promiscuity than heterosexual men. At the level of biological instinct, probably both are equally strongly inclined to the purely mechanical release of sexual energy – more strongly in general than women, for whom sexual activity is widely agreed to be less driven and immediate in kind, and more dependent on personal and relational conditions. However, there are at least two special factors which may have made homosexual men statistically more promiscuous than heterosexuals. The first is that in the absence of opportunities in ordinary life for meeting other gay people, and without accepted social structures within which 'courting' can take place, homosexual couples tend to move more rapidly to sexual expression than heterosexual couples. The second factor is the comparative availability of promiscuous sex. For a heterosexual man, finding a woman to have sex with is likely to be a time-consuming and expensive activity. For homosexual men, at least in an urban area, finding another man for the impersonal, rapid release of sexual energy is likely to be an easy matter, however dangerous and demeaning it may be. For some it becomes a compulsive addiction.

Assumptions about promiscuous gay activity have bolstered hostility towards homosexuals in general, especially among conservative Christians, whose anti-gay literature frequently includes startling statistics and lurid descriptions of extreme sexual practices intended to generate or reinforce general revulsion. In matters of propaganda fine distinctions are not made: gay people are placarded as those 'who do that kind of thing'. To some extent, especially in the past, this negative, marginalizing attitude may have been internalized by gay people themselves, who found themselves living up – or down – to precisely the expectations others have of them. It is particularly unfortunate and unfair that whereas until recently most stable homosexual relationships have been secret and invisible to society, so that this 'model' was rarely seen, promiscuous homosexual behaviour or behaviour involving minors was frequently reported in the media, and so readily became associated in the public mind with homosexuality in general. Homosexuals are still assumed by many to be promiscuous or paedophile by nature, because for so many years that assumption was pedalled by the media, and no other model of being gay was ever seen.

It is worth noting that even today this particular catch-22 can also affect bishops. Bishops who are known to have negative views about homosexuality naturally do not receive the confidences of their gay clergy, and are likely to remain unaware of their existence. The only gay clergy they get to know about are the ones who get into trouble. They are then prone to view all gay people in the same light – which bolsters the negative views they held in the first place. I have met two or three bishops whose thinking was very clearly conditioned in this way by having to deal with errant clergy. Several bishops seem quite unaware of the numbers of gay clergy in their dioceses who live in good, sustaining and faithful gay partnerships. One or two have even announced that they have no practising gay clergy in their diocese at all, to the grim amusement of the 'non-existent' clergy in question!

Statistics about promiscuous sexual activity are revealing. In the years when such information was gathered, police reports showed that around half of those arrested for homosexual activity in public places were married men. This much-ignored evidence has an obvious implication. It is clear that a large number of men who were predominantly or at least significantly homosexual in orientation, having adopted for whatever reason the course of marriage, have been driven to seek satisfaction for their true sexual nature in this way. It is fair to ask how many of them would have been saved from this situation if building a decent same-sex partnership had ever been presented to them as a viable option. It is very much to be hoped that increasing acceptance of gay relationships will bring about a corresponding decrease in the phenomenon of 'lavender marriage' and the misery it has brought to so many families.

Other statistics have shown that, as one might expect, the incidence of promiscuous activity among gay men falls dramatically when they enter into a stable relationship. This proves that gay monogamy, no less than heterosexual marriage, effectively fulfils its Prayer Book function as a 'remedy against sin'. Again it is fair to ask how many gay men in the past would have been saved from involvement in promiscuous and compulsive sex if they had had the chance of living and loving in a stable relationship.

Nevertheless, temptation clearly remains for gay people in a committed partnership, as well as for single or celibate or married homosexuals or bisexuals, who are aware of the easy availability of casual sex on the gay scene. Someone in this situation is not helped by the relatively light view taken of casual sex in much of the gay subculture, and even in some Christian gay publications such as those criticized in the last chapter. It is true, of course, that far more is involved in the concept of faith-fulness to another person than sexual fidelity alone. It is also true that sexual sin is not the worst sin, and that an act of sexual infidelity need not mean the destruction of a relationship. But we need to counter the idea that pro-miscuous gay sex is somehow more excusable than pro-miscuous heterosexual sex, or that it is a morally irrelevant expression of biological need ('little more than sneezing', as I once heard it described). Nor will it do to suggest that a Christian sexual relationship or a Christian liturgy of commitment may or may not involve vows of sexual fidelity, or to imply that a sexually open relationship can be as valid as a sexually exclusive one.

This is not merely a matter of rules but of personal and spiritual realities. As has already been observed at the practical level, within a heterosexual marriage or a homosexual partnership, couples who begin by allowing sexual openness regularly find that it ends in jealousy, hurt and destruction. Christians above all cannot lose sight of the fact that sex is not to be isolated from the totality of who and what we are. Jack Dominian, who has written powerfully about the relationship between sex and personal integrity, strongly advocates that the Church should do all it can to encourage faithful relationships among homosexuals as a way to integration and spiritual maturity. He observes that there is psychological as well as theological truth in Pauls' observation that sex always has spiritual consequences for the person, whether for good or ill. Sex has its own dynamic; it always tends to give life and 'make love', but where it is torn away from all possibility of love in personal commitment it tends ultimately to futility and the disintegration of the person.

Jim Cotter in an essay entitled *The Shaping of Gay Relationships* remarks, quoting Harry Williams on chastity:

> It is precisely because sex is so powerful a desire that it can make a takeover bid and dominate our lives. It is precisely because the person may be highly sexed and know the power of the junkie and the prostitute within that the quality of the relationship with the other needs to be kept central ... 'Emotional chastity consists of the attempt to discover our own genuine deep feelings and of being loyal to them even when temporary feelings of an opposite but more superficial kind bang noisily within us.' We may have to discern in life not only what is the lesser of two evils, but

also what is the greatest of two goods. And that will involve times of saying No for the sake of times of saying Yes.

As I said at the start, we all inhabit glass houses and there are times when we all fail and need forgiveness, if only in the matter of 'looking lustfully'. To recognize this and to treat it compassionately is not the same as to abandon Christian ethics and pretend that chastity, in the true sense of sexual fidelity and integrity, does not matter. It does matter, and within the conditions of the secular gay scene it is important for gay Christians to witness to it.

Being Exemplary: Clergy in Homosexual Relationships

We have, therefore, to say that in our considered judgement the clergy cannot claim the liberty to enter into sexually active homophile relationships. Because of the distinctive nature of their calling, status and consecration, to allow such a claim on their part would be seen as placing that way of life in all respects on a par with heterosexual marriage as the reflection of God's purposes in creation. The church cannot accept such a parity and remain faithful to the insights which God has given through scripture, tradition and reasoned reflection on experience.

This was the conclusion of the bishops' judgment in *Issues* on the question of homosexual relationships and the clergy. Earlier I focused on the crucial issue as to what the bishops mean by the 'imparity' between homosexual and heterosexual relationships, and why this is seen as a deciding factor in respect of the clergy's 'exemplary' function. The bishops earlier in the report make it clear that they do not consider a faithful homosexual relationship a vicious or morally inferior way of life; otherwise they could not recommend the acceptance of such relationships into congregations, nor say that such couples can be a 'blessing to the world around them, and … achieve great, even heroic sacrifice and devotion'. The 'imparity' cannot reside in the impossibility of childbirth, since there is no bar on clergy in infertile marriages. Even if the bishops regard homosexuality as a handicap, there is no bar on handicapped clergy. Nor are celibate clergy debarred in the Anglican Church, despite the fact that such a state arguably flies more directly in the face of 'God's purposes declared in creation'. So why, having concluded after a reasoned reassessment of Scripture, tradition and experience, that for lay homosexuals a faithful, stable, permanent relationship may be God's call and their way to holiness, do the bishops say this cannot be so among the clergy?

The ruling is linked to the statement that clergy are called to exemplify an ideal, but that (in this mysterious and unspecified way) clergy in a homosexual partnership fall short of the ideal and therefore cannot be a good example. Of course for most heterosexuals faithful marriage is the ideal – and there are faithful married clergy to exemplify it. For those who are called to celibacy, clergy or laypeople, faithful celibacy is the ideal, and there are faithful celibate clergy to exemplify it. I have argued that for homosexuals who are not called to celibacy faithful monogamous partnership is the ideal (and in the case of lay people the bishops seem to accept it) – and there are in fact faithful clergy partnerships to exemplify it too. But this, the bishops say, is wrong.

The position is all the more ironic because if there is a single group of people who desperately need an ideal and role-models to exemplify it, it is gay people. Frankly, it seems a doubtful proposition that many heterosexual parishioners look to the local vicar and his or her spouse as their icon of married bliss. It seems unlikely too that very many model themselves on clergy in following a celibate life. On the other hand, it is the experience of many clergy in gay relationships who have allowed this to be known, that they rapidly draw a large clientèle of other gay people who cannot find the kind of positive Christian counselling they need anywhere else. In this situation, more than any other I know, the role model of the priest really is indispensable, and becomes a rock on which others can build. But is is intolerably hard for clergy to fill this need when their own support from the Church is withdrawn.

The bishops' conclusion, and their continued hard-line on the matter since the publication of *Issues*, is dismaying for another reason. Many bishops know perfectly well, and in private fully accept, that some of their clergy are in gay relationships. Not a few bishops themselves have been in homosexual relationships in the past, and in secret some are still. There are now many clergy in the church however who have rejected such secrecy and

insisted on being honest about their private lives with
their ordaining and employing bishops, with those who
selected them for training, with their training college
principals, and with others in authority. Most clergy who
have taken the risk of being open with their bishops about
being in a gay relationship have found support – but only
in private. In public the backing is almost always withdrawn. It is extraordinary that so many bishops have
constantly allowed this private support to be publicly
negated under the anonymity of collective, official episcopal statements. When *Issues* was first published a
number of bishops contacted their gay clergy to assure
them that it didn't really mean what it said. That was
kind, but hardly admirable. But it is typical of the double-
think that infects the Church, and especially its leadership, on this particular issue.

In the Preface to *Issues* it was underlined that it was
intended to be a transitional document to promote an
educational process. In fact what was meant to be transitional soon crystallised into a policy document which has
remained in place for twenty years, such that all who
want to be ordained have to promise to 'abide' by it as a
matter of discipline. It has thus effectively helped stop
the education process it was meant to promote. While
society has learned and moved on towards acceptance
even of gay marriage, the Church has remained static or
even moved backwards. The toxic fear, secrecy and
hypocrisy which surround the subject make it too hard
for those who know the truth to tell the truth. No
genuine education process will begin in the Church until
the bishops in particular begin to allow 'what is whis-

pered in private rooms to be shouted from the house-tops'. This means, among other things, taking their episcopal teaching office seriously, and finding the courage to let even 'difficult' conservative Evangelicals among their colleagues and their clergy know their real views. The Gospel does not allow a divergence between public and private moralities, and political expediency is not a Christian virtue – rather the opposite. The unity of the Church should not be bought at the price of hypocrisy, or of scapegoating those who are seldom in a position to defend themselves. If, as all the private evidence shows, the majority of bishops in the church are in fact quietly willing to accept and support their gay clergy, they should be prepared to stand up themselves and in Christ's name say why. They may even find – as many gay clergy have found – that by doing so respect is won and opposition melts away.

Dr Ben Fletcher, in a survey of stress among the clergy, wrote in conclusion, with gay clergy particularly in view:

> It is surely now necessary for the Church to change policy. Evidence shows that committed relationships provide partners with a protective buffer against stress and illness ... What is needed surely is a positive ethic for committed and stable homosexual relationships analogous to heterosexual marriage. The church needs to encourage a lifelong commitment between homosexual partners in much the same way it does between heterosexual partners. (*Clergy Under Stress*, p 117)

Liturgies, Recognition and Acceptance

The most positive thing the Church can do for any couple to encourage their lifelong commitment is to offer them a liturgy which affirms their vows and celebrates, blesses and strengthens their love for one another. If, as the bishops affirmed even in *Issues*, a faithful gay relationship can be a 'source of blessing' to the partners and to others around them, what possible warrant is there for refusing to give it the blessing of the Church? Nevertheless, following the introduction of civil partnerships for gay people, the bishops in an official statement of 2006 explicitly forbade the use of any form of public vows, exchange of rings or blessing, and restricted clergy to offering private prayers with the couple outside the church building.

So, in default of any official provision, inevitably a number of unofficial liturgies, or liturgies from other churches, are being used with increasing frequency. For the reasons I have already discussed I believe that any liturgy which is used to ratify and bless a sexual relationship ought to be undergirded by a strong sacramental theology of sex, and for that reason I do not think the Church could ever approve the use of such a service, any more than it could provide a form of marriage, unless it rested on similar vows of permanence, fidelity, and stability. It is extremely encouraging to know that gay people who approach the Church for blessings almost invariably want their relationship to rest on vows of this kind.

It is important to remember, of course, that the church does not marry anyone. The Anglican understanding of marriage is that the couple themselves are the ministers of the sacrament. The church hears and approves the promises which the partners make to one another, and adds its declaration of God's blessing to their commitment. By doing so it also implies its willingness to support in every practical and spiritual way possible the keeping of that commitment. Every mature married couple knows, and the bishops emphasize in their Statement, that a successful marriage cannot and must not be a private, inward-looking arrangement – 'selfishness for two' – but depends on a whole network of supporting relationships with those around. The marriage service itself asks God to give the couple grace to minister to others, and to be a witness to Christ's saving love in the world: 'It is the strength of this many-dimensioned partnership which will make them a more effective means of grace together than they would have been apart.'

An officially endorsed liturgy of blessing for gay couples, as well as affirming and expressing God's love for the couple themselves, would help immeasurably toward creating in church and society the same acceptance and support for gay partnerships that any marriage needs to flourish. Among the sadnesses often imposed on gay people, especially in the past, has been the inability to celebrate their relationship publicly and need to keep their love secret from family or colleagues or friends. As Sanderson notes in *Making Gay Relationships Work*, this enforced secrecy robs the relationship of dignity, denies it space to grow, and deprives it of the kind of support network that we recognize is essential to a marriage.

Maximizing the possibility of openness and sharing is as
vital to the health of a gay relationship as to any other.
Heterosexual Christians of goodwill need to recognize
the heroic level of courage and cost which may be
involved for some gay people, especially those with a
religious and traditional family background, in overcom-
ing the fear of 'coming out'. If they are in a position to
help, there is plenty of help they can give. For homosexual partnerships simple things that married couples
take for granted – joint invitations, anniversary cards,
inquiries about one's partner – become immensely
important signs of affirmation. The whole point is that,
whatever one calls it, the relationship is analogous to a
marriage and should be reacted to in the same way. There
will be no reality behind the bishops' vaguely urging
'acceptance' of gay people by churches unless this is
taken on board and some real liturgical provision is
made.

One of the most curious arguments against recognizing gay partnerships or extending civil marriage to gay
people is that it would constitute a threat to 'family
values' or to the social order at large. This seems highly
illogical. In what possible sense does a gay couple making
lifelong vows to one another threaten or destabilise heterosexual couples who do the same? Theologically and
socially the acceptance of same-sex partners in covenant
relationships does not overturn the institution of marriage and the family, it actually affirms it by extending it.
At the pragmatic level, society benefits when people are
committed to caring for one another, and are not left
alone and reliant on the state. When civil partnerships

were first being mooted, the editors of the Economist made the same point in respect of the need we all have to be cared for till death us do part:

> It is important to support the legal recognition of same-sex couples as a matter of social justice. As things stand, a gay couple may live together for years, but when one dies the surviving partner may have very few rights over their home, property, or even the funeral arrangements. The experience of AIDS produced countless heartbreaking stories of gay partners, one of whom had nursed the other through sickness, being separated from one another at the deathbed and funeral by hostile parents, who in law were accorded the final right to the body of a son whom they might have rejected and ignored for years.

The ultimate importance of recognition, however, goes well beyond questions of social security or secular justice. For gay people there is a deeper, more inward wound to be healed, and a deeper freedom to be won, from an immemorial legacy of fear and repression, much of it generated and sustained by religion. At the most profound level it is a matter of regaining self-respect. Homosexuals have long internalized society's rejection, and it is only society's – and even more the Church's – full acceptance and blessing which can heal it. Andrew Sullivan describes the importance of establishing a recognized form of same-sex monogamy in these terms:

It is not simply about 'taming' or civilizing' gay men. It is also the deepest means for the liberation of homosexuals, providing them with the only avenue for sexual and emotional development that can integrate them as equal human beings and remove from them the hideous historic option of choosing between their joy and their dignity. It is about deepening and widening and strengthening the possibility of true intimacy between two human beings. (*Love Undetectable* p. 67)

In other words, it is about how gay people, like everyone else, can best realize their fullest humanity, their making in the image of God. The Church understands marriage as a covenant within which two people are called to find their truest selves by giving themselves away in love to one another. As we have seen, it is a 'mystery' or sacrament of God because it potentially reflects the mystery of self-giving love which is at the heart of the Trinity: the dynamic, creative interchange of love which binds persons in one, yet such that they become more fully themselves. At the same time, the couple are a cell in the Body of Christ, the Church, where we are all learning, often joyfully but sometimes painfully and sacrificially, to live in love with each other, to understand and enter into the experience of each other, so as also to model and reflect at the level of our common life the unity-in-diversity which is the life of God.

So in different ways at different levels, both marriage and the Church are God-given training-grounds for learning Trinitarian love. Both can 'work' equally for homosexual people – if they are allowed in – because homosexual people are no less made in God's image than heterosexuals, and no less capable of loving in his image. For that reason among many others Eugene Rogers, in a meticulous study of sexuality in relation to the Christian tradition, concluded that the explicit inclusion of homosexual couples within that Body is crucial not only to the health of homosexuals, but to the health and completeness of the Church itself.

> Gay and lesbian unions can build up the Church as well as straight marriages do, with or without children in both cases. Certainly lesbian and gay relationships can exhibit an *égoïsm à deux*, but they need not, any more that straight ones do. Marriage forms that included gay and lesbian couples would make clear that their unions, too, are from and for the larger community – indeed, if the kingdom of God is like a wedding feast, it is thus that they too represent the Trinity. (*Sexuality and the Christian Body* p. 273)

4

POSTSCRIPT 2012

An undertaking has been given by the British government that civil marriage will become available to gay couples by 2015. That will be the clearest possible signal that gay people are accepted in this society on a fully equal basis. It will be the culmination of a long and hard fight for respect and equality that began in the fifties and won its first major victory with the decriminalisation of homosexuality in Britain in 1967 – a move supported by the then Archbishop Michael Ramsey and by his predecessor Geoffrey Fisher, as well as by the great majority of the hierarchy of the Church of England. It is no less than a tragedy for Christianity in this country that since that time, whereas the process of recognizing and integrating gay people has steadily continued in society at large, the most visible and vocal obstacle to that continuing process has been the Church, which since 1967 has opposed every further step forward that has been taken. The bishops who voted for the Resolution on Human Sexuality at the Lambeth Conference of 1998; those who opposed the Equalization of the Age of Consent bill and the adoption of European Human Rights legislation in respect of gay people; those who attempted to wreck the passage through Parliament of the bill to establish civil partnerships; and now those who are opposing the introduction of civil marriage – they have ensured that the

Church of the twenty-first century in this country is now perceived as the Enemy Number One of gay people. They have guaranteed that this particular section of the population, which still needs more than most to be brought in from the margins, will be the least likely to come within its doors.

I said in the Preface that one of the chief reasons for the failure of the Church to allow change has been the attempt to keep on board extremely homophobic Anglican provinces which back harsh and sometimes deadly laws against gay people in their own countries. Such is the political fear of the Communion breaking up that very few words have been spoken against this situation, and practically nothing done: blackmail and bigotry have been met with a policy of appeasement and capitulation. Meanwhile the American and Canadian churches have been condemned and 'sanctioned' by the Archbishop of Canterbury for speaking the truth and following conscience by blessing gay partnerships and ordaining openly gay bishops. This is morality turned upside down; and the inevitable result is that people of goodwill with a concern for justice and truth turn away from the Church in disgust.

Almost as long as it has existed, the Church has been directly responsible for evils and injustices committed against gay people, and it is responsible for them still. Appalling atrocities have been perpetrated on homosexuals by the Church, or in the name of the Church, or as in Nazi Germany, with the tacit connivance of the Church. Yet there is still not a glimmer of repentance; rather the opposite – an arrogant restatement of 'traditional' exclusion and contempt. Nor should the bishops imagine that the ugly words and deeds of homophobia in this country and around the world can somehow be isolated from their own words and votes. They continue to defend the attitudes and ideology which undergird prejudice, and they continue to bear the heaviest responsibility for it.

5

QUESTIONS

Introduction

What is your initial reaction to the words 'homosexual', 'lesbian', 'gay'? Before reading this book where did you stand on the 'gay issue' in the Church?

Were you aware of the Lambeth Conference resolution on sexuality in 1998, or the bishops' Statement of 1991, *Issues in Human Sexuality?* Does what is said about them here surprise you?

Why do you think some gay people are strongly opposed to this author's view that marriage is appropriate to gay relationships as well as to heterosexual relationships?

What do you think of the author's view that admitting gay couples into the sacrament of marriage is similar to admitting women into the sacrament of ordination?

Do you think that there are any gay couples in your church? Would you know? If not, why not?

How do you react to the author's claim that in asking to have their relationships accepted, most gay people only want what everyone else takes for granted?

Is it Scriptural?

What is your reaction to the story of Simon? If you had been in the vicar's place, what would you have said?

Do you agree with the author's claim that it is unfair to take the bible literally on the subject of homosexuality, but not on the subject of divorce and remarriage, or the subordination of women?

How useful is Old Testament material which mentions homosexuality in helping us to decide about it today?

Read Romans 1:18 – end. Does the author's commentary on the passage seem fair?

Does it make any difference that Paul seems to think only in terms of homosexual acts committed by basically heterosexual people, and does not take into account the fact that for some people sexuality is not a matter of choice?

Why is it significant that Jesus and Paul do not link their call to faithfulness in marriage to practical reasons of childbearing and family stability, but to spiritual ones?

Do you think it is true, as the author interprets Paul and Jesus as saying, that 'sexual union always has spiritual consequences'?

Do you agree that a same-sex couple can 'signify the union between Christ and the Church' in the same way as a heterosexual couple? If not, what is the difference?

Can you conceive of a 'distinctively Christian' gay relationship? What would be distinctive about it?

Is It Moral?

How important is it to the moral argument that two male or two female bodies do not physically fit together?

The author notes a strong reaction in many people against anal intercourse in particular. Does it make any difference to the argument whether we are talking about manual, oral or anal homosexual sex? Is it more morally acceptable if heterosexual couples also do the same things with each other?

Why do you think lesbianism seems to arouse less opposition in society than male gay sex?

What do you think of the author's comparison of the use of the body in gay sex with a handicapped person writing with his feet?

Do you agree that the question whether homosexuality is caused by genes or by upbringing is irrelevant to the argument about accepting gay relationships?

Do you agree that the fact that a gay couple cannot have children makes no difference to the argument?

How would you feel if your child told you he or she was gay? What would you say and do?

The bishops' statement *Issues in Human Sexuality* says homosexual couples can be 'a blessing to the world around them'. How?

Would you agree with the bishops that a homosexual relationship is necessarily less valid than a heterosexual one?

Do you think it is true that a man and a woman complement each other in a way that two men or two women never can?

This author is strongly opposed to using the term 'friendship' for a homosexual relationship, and prefers 'monogamy', 'covenant' or 'marriage'. Why?

How do you feel about using the words 'marriage' and 'monogamy' of a relationship between two men or two women?

The author is very positive and traditional in his attitude to marriage. Is he right? Or do you side with Elizabeth Stuart, believing marriage is based on slavery, and that gay people would be better off with freer forms of relationship?

What do you think of the author's view that sex, gay or straight, is best kept within a faithful, lifelong relationship? Do you agree that this is a more important question than the particular question of gay relationships?

Do you agree with the author's view that a radically liberationist view of sex is 'dangerous'? Why – or why not?

Is It Achievable?

Are you surprised that so many homosexual relationships seem to last?

Do you agree that homosexual men are not inherently more promiscuous than heterosexual men? Do you agree that women (straight or lesbian) are generally less promiscuous than men?

How do you account for the fact that so many of the men arrested for having gay sex in public places are married?

What advice would you give to a person who is equally attracted to both sexes?

Do you agree that promiscuous sexual activity 'tends ultimately to futility and the disintegration of the person'?

Are there grounds for the Church accepting lay people in a same-sex relationship, but not clergy?

How would you react if you discovered your vicar/ priest/minister was in a gay relationship?

If you were a bishop or other senior Church leader, and one of your clergy told you he or she was gay, how would you react?

How would you feel if you were invited to a blessing service for a gay couple or if you heard one was going to take place in your church?

Do you know any same-sex couples? If so, how have they influenced your view?

Do you think blessing same-sex partnerships or opening marriage to gay couples would threaten marriage and family life? If so, how?

Do you agree that the church itself would benefit from public recognition of same-sex couples?

How do you feel about the Church of England bishops' record of opposing homosexual partnerships, an equal age of consent, equal employment rights, and civil marriage?

Do you agree that the Church should recognize its own part in the oppression of gay people and seek ways to redeem it?

SELECT BIBLIOGRAPHY

The Gloucester Report published as *Homosexual Relationships – A Contribution to Discussion* (London, Church Information Office, 1979)

Issues in Human Sexuality: A Statement by the House of Bishops (London, Church House Publishing, 1991)

Some Issues in Human Sexuality: A Guide to the Debate (London, Church House Publishing, 2003)

Balch, D.L., *Homosexuality, Science and the 'Plain Sense' of Scripture* (Grand Rapids, Eerdmans, 2000)

Bellis, A.O. and Hufford, T.L., *Science, Scripture and Homosexuality* (Cleveland, Pilgrim, 2002)

Boswell, J., *Christianity, Social Tolerance and Homosexuality* (Chicago, University of Chicago, 1980)

Bradshaw, T. (ed.), *The Way Forward? Christian Voices on Homosexuality and the Church* (London, Hodder and Stoughton, 1998)

Brett, P. *Rethinking Christian Attitudes to Sex* (Colchester, University of Essex, 1991)

Cotter, J. (ed.) *Exploring Lifestyles: An Introduction to Services of Blessing for Gay Couples* (London, Gay Christian Movement, 1980)

Cotter, J., *Freedom and Framework: The Shaping of Gay Relationships* (London, Gay Christian Movement, 1978)

Countryman, L.W., *Dirt, Greed and Sex* (London, SCM, 1988)

Doe, M., *Seeking the Truth in Love* (London, Darton, Longman and Todd, 2000)

Dominian, J., *Sexual Integrity* (London, Mowbray, 1987)

Dormor, D. and Morris, J. (eds.), *An Acceptable Sacrifice? Homosexuality and the Church* (London, SPCK, 2007)

Fletcher, B., *Clergy Under Stress* (London, Mowbray, 1990)

Gagnon, Robert A. J., *The Bible and Homosexual Practice: Texts and Hermeneutics* (Nashville, Abingdon, 2001)

Gibson, P., *Discerning the Word: The Bible and Homosexuality in Anglican Debate* (Toronto, Anglican Book Centre, 2000)

Heskins, J., *Unheard Voices* (London, Darton, Longman and Todd, 2001)

John, J., 'Homosexuality and the Bible' in *Widening the Horizons* (London, Christian Action, 1990)

Kelly, K.T., *New Directions in Sexual Ethics* (London, Geoffrey Chapman, 1998)

McCord Adams, M., 'Sex and the Sins of the Fathers' in *Radical Christian Voices and Practice: Essays in Honour of Christopher Rowland* (Oxford, OUP, 2012)

McNeill, J., *The Church and the Homosexual* (New York, NextYear, 1985)

Moore, G., *The Body in Context: Sex and Catholicism* (London, SCM, 1992)

    A Question of Truth: Christianity and Homosexuality (London, Continuum, 2003)

Nelson, J., *The Intimate Connection: Male Sexuality, Masculine Spirituality* (London, SPCK, 1992)

Rogers, E.F., *Sexuality and the Christian Body* (Oxford, Blackwell, 1999)

Rogers, J., *Jesus, the Bible and Homosexuality: Explode the Myths, Heal the Church* (Louisville, KY, Westminster, John Knox, 2006)

Rowland, C. and Roberts, J, *The Bible for Sinners* (London, SPCK, 2008)

Sanderson, T., *Making Gay Relationships Work* (London, Other Way, 1990)

Scroggs, R., *The New Testament and Homosexuality* (Minneapolis, Fortress, 1983)

Stuart, E., *Daring to Speak Love's Name* (London, Hamish Hamilton, 1992)

    Just Good Friends (London, Mowbray, 1999)

Sullivan, A., *Virtually Normal* (London, Picador, 1995)

    Same-Sex Marriage: Pro and Con. A Reader (New York, Random House, 1997)

Love Undetectable (London, Chatto and Windus, 1998)

Tessina, T., *Gay Relationships* (Los Angeles, Tarcher, 1989)

Thatcher, A., *Liberating Sex: A Christian Sexual Theology* (London, SPCK, 1993)

Thévenot, X., *Homosexualités Masculines et Morale Chretienne* (Paris, Cerf, 1985)

Vasey, M., *Evangelical Christians and Gay Rights* (Nottingham, Grove Books, 1991)

Strangers and Friends: A New Exploration of Homosexuality and the Bible (London, Hodder and Stoughton, 1995)

Wenham, G., 'Homosexuality in the Bible' in T. Higton (ed.), *Sexuality and the Church* (Action for Biblical Witness to our Nation) (Eastbourne, Kingsway, 1987)

Williams, R. 'Towards a Theology for Lesbian and Gay Marriage' in *The Anglican Theological Review* (Vol. LXXII, no. 2, 1990)

Williams, R., *The Body's Grace* (London, LGCM 2002)

Introduction to *Speaking Love's Name: Homosexuality: Some Catholic and Socialist Reflections* (London, The Jubilee Group, 1988)

Unpublished letters to Dr D. Pitt on same-sex relationships at http://www.thinkinganglicans.org.uk/archives/003361.html

Wink, W., *Homosexuality and Christian Faith: Questions of Conscience for the Churches* (Minneapolis, Fortress, 1999)